she just wants to forget

r.h. Sin

Andrews McMeel
PUBLISHING®

other books by r.h. Sin

Whiskey Words & a Shovel

Whiskey Words & a Shovel II

Whiskey Words & a Shovel III

Rest in the Mourning

A Beautiful Composition of Broken

Algedonic

She Felt Like Feeling Nothing

Planting Gardens in Graves

Planting Gardens in Graves II

Planting Gardens in Graves III

We Hope This Reaches You in Time
with Samantha King Holmes

Empty Bottles Full of Stories
with R. M. Drake

you are, you are II.

I have something to tell you
One last thing to say here
I have something I need you to know
Before I go
Before we part
Before this ends

You are more than you probably know
You are valuable, just in case you forgot
You are . . . wait hold on . . .

There's a knock at the door . . .

For some odd reason I didn't look through the
peephole, strange feeling I guess. This moment of
understanding hovered over my mind as if I knew
who was standing on the other side of the door. It
was raining that night, the thunder cracking against
the window like a whip. The sky marked by the light
of skyscraper buildings. I opened the door without
hesitation and there she was. A bold statement of
strength and energy. A source of divine motion

whenever moving. She stood there soaked in rain and that's maybe why I didn't notice the sadness at first because the tears she cried hid behind the appearance of rain water dripping from her face. She never needed me, she was capable of getting to where she needed to get to emotionally on her own but in that moment, I knew I had to be there for her.

I think this is when she actually entered my life. This would be the moment that would change everything. "It's crazy how sometimes you have to be destroyed to be made anew," she said. "Everything happens for a reason, just like this moment. I do believe that what you're dealing with will pass," I responded.

And so, I wrote this for her, for you because you are worth it.

scene thirty-nine.

I wrote this for the woman in search of a reminder of who she's always been. A reminder of who she was before the heartache, before the madness. I wrote this for the woman who has seen a large share of heartbreak, the woman who finds herself tired of being strong, tired of standing in the middle of the storm. I wrote this for the woman who continues to demand more even in the eyes of those who would rather do less. I wrote this for her because she . . . you . . . deserve it. You have been through so much and yet you continue to hold your head high, and though you've been constantly disappointed, you find new and rare ways to hold on to this sort of hope that feels more like magic. You are powerful even in moments where weakness chases you. You are mighty even though your struggles stand like giants in the doorway of your happiness. I wrote this for you because you are a remarkable woman.

There's a light that lives within you that could rival the sun and a glow in your eyes that could distract from the moon on its darkest night. You, this remarkable and rare occurrence, unlike anything most have ever seen. You, this beautiful wonder, a muse to artists and writers like me. Living loud when the world wishes to silence the melody that has been cradled in your heart. Unapologetic with the intention of being greater than the world would have you be. I wrote this for you in hopes of encouraging you to continue toward everything you truly deserve. I wrote these words for the woman in search of a reminder of who she's always been.

This is specifically for the woman who feels stuck. I wrote these words for the woman who is tired of fighting for someone who only wants to fight her. Every letter here was meant to form words that will speak to the strong women who are tired of wasting their energy, choosing someone who never chooses them. I wrote this for her, for you. I wrote this for the woman who is looking for a sign. I wrote these sentences for the woman who no longer knows what she wants to do or maybe she's decided to stay even though she knows leaving will save her soul. That woman is you and she is tired of the confusion and the delusion and of living in a horrific illusion. The truth is, you're just that powerful. You're just that strong. You have the ability to hold on even when it hurts. You're tired of loving someone who refuses to acknowledge your worth. It's not easy, I know, but in order to grow closer to what you deserve, you'll need to walk away from the person who no longer deserves you. I wrote this because you're ready to read it and I hope these words encourage you to move on.

scene forty.

There's something about the day that seems longer than usual whenever you're dealing with sadness and or fighting through a struggle that would appear not meant for you to survive. It's days like this where you feel the most tested, tired from the night before. Weary from the evenings of no rest, lying in bed staring at the ceiling in hopes of finding sleep. Incapable of putting your mind to peace, you tumble through the night as if your eyes were closed and your hands were tied as you attempt to navigate down a hill of problems. The night bleeds into the morning sky and your eyes go from dancing around the stars to witnessing the moon vanish to make way for the sun.

There's something about the day that seems a bit harder than the rest. You've been trying your best to ignore it all but you fall flat on your face without warning and no one is there to witness this. No one is there to lend a helping hand but somehow you end up reaching for yourself because it's always been that way, hasn't it? You've been all you've had since the beginning. Your parents weren't much help, your struggles began early on and here you are as a result of everything that has happened to you. Here you are today in this moment, struggling through all the things that you have no control over. Your father, inconsistent. His hands barely there to protect you, his hands barely there to shield you and so you had to learn about wolves on your own. He was never present enough and somehow that led you to entertaining relationships with men who were just as inconsistent as he's always been. Your mother dropped the ball on informing you of what being a woman would mean. She fell short of teaching you those lessons and so you found yourself rogue on any mission that would hopefully lead you to some sort of understanding of yourself. The teachers of your lessons were devils pretending that they could provide some sense of heaven and you believed it because you grew weary of experiencing hell. You wanted something different and so you listened because what they said was the opposite of what you knew but you didn't know that they would simply do the opposite of what they promised. Honestly, you figured them out to be liars but even then you held on to this hope that one day their words would somehow catch up to their actions. It never does, though, and moving on is so slow. You feel it in your heart and even worse in your soul. All of this because your parents refused to let you know that you yourself are way too valuable to be dealing with some guy with some nerves with mostly pain in his words that sound like love at first. You feel it to your core, all because your parents refused to teach you and so these men would eventually teach you that you are unworthy of everything you actually deserve. All because your parents refused to teach you and so these men would eventually teach you to settle because what you're looking for shouldn't have been looked for.

scene forty-one.

It was never hard to tell; I think deep down she always knew that there was something going on. Even if you decided to say nothing, even when you thought you were so skilled at hiding whatever it was. Deep down, she always knew and yet she decided to say nothing. She decided to say nothing because maybe the truth was something she wasn't ready to face. Maybe she knew that coming to terms with what she'd discover would force her to do everything that she was avoiding all along. They say everything done in the darkness will somehow find it's moment in the light and this is exactly what happened even when you don't know that it has. Even when you think that for some odd reason you'll never be found out. She knows, she knows, she knows and she'll say nothing for now because right now the lies ironically feel a bit safer. As strange as it may be, the lies you told, the lies she chose to believe have prevented her from facing a horrible truth. She knows and one day when she's ready, she'll move forward from you . . .

scene forty-two.

She was tired but she was powerful. She loved you
and yet it was never enough because you were never
enough for her. She was weary and yet she continued
to move, refusing to stand still. Realizing that
standing next to you would ruin the opportunity
to go after the things that would otherwise bring
her peace. She represented something so grand,
something so special. Something so rare and still you
decided to treat her as if her everything was nothing
and so she began the process of cleansing herself
of what she initially felt for you. The woman you
chose to overlook and neglect decided to love herself
rather than continue falling for someone who would
never catch her.

scene forty—three.

I think there's this part of you that remains hidden.
There's a side of you that most people rarely see.
You've buried that part of you deep like roots
beneath trees, undiscovered by those who were
never willing to search for you. There's way too
much depth in your soul and those too lazy to
explore your extra layers have all come up short
and you willingly allow it, you don't bother to tell
them that there's more because you know that not
everyone deserves all of which you have to offer.
You've hidden so much because you're tired of the
betrayal that follows behind those who don't deserve
passage upon your heart's bridge. So much of you
left to be discovered by someone who doesn't have
to be told where to go. Someone who knows what to
do and how to treat you without hurting you in the
process. I think there's this part of you that will mean
the world to the right person, but until then, you
will always mean the world to yourself and there is
nothing wrong with protecting your light from those
who will only represent darkness.

Hello, my name is Reuben but you know me as r.h. Sin and while I have your attention here in this moment, I just wanted to take this time to apologize to you on behalf of anyone who has ever hurt your soul. I'm well aware that you may not have gotten any closure or clarity from all those failed relationships and people who have constantly taken you for granted but I wanted to say sorry because even though we're strangers and we've never crossed paths, I believe here and now that you deserve so much more than what you've had in the past. I believe in you and your ability to love without condition and while it feels like a curse, it's truly a gift that belongs to you. A gift that will one day be appreciated by the one who is willing to match everything you'll provide. I want to apologize to you but at the same time I'd like to remind you that you are amazing, you are someone worth getting to know and I am grateful for the opportunity to speak with you here and now, in this moment.

your sister III.

You allowed her into our home without giving it a second thought. I must admit I had my reservations but who am I to stand between family, who am I to prevent you from acting on your heart? I fell in love with you because of the kindness that dwells in your soul and so we became her temporary home. She and her child, your nephew, my nephew too. We allowed her into our home with ease and so it pains me to think about how far she's gone to alienate you and me as if we did nothing to help. I thought sisters were supposed to move in love, I thought older sisters were supposed to be protective, supportive and loving. I thought more of her, I believed in her, and my mistake was thinking that she had the same heart as you. I was wrong . . . we were wrong, but life goes on I guess.

family & friends?

They always want to bring up your mistakes as if you've done nothing right. It's like no one's there until you fuck up, it's like no one cares until there's a moment provided for them to point a finger at you as if you're the only one to blame. Insane to think that your accomplishments will often go ignored by the very people who should be proud of you for being more than they're willing to give you credit for. There's this concept of family and friends that isn't always true and sometimes those relationships fail to live up to what they're defined to be. You are special even when they choose not to acknowledge it. You have a good heart, no matter what they think. You've done an amazing job at being you and learning more about yourself without the guidance of those who were supposed to hold your hand through the storm and you've grown because of it. You are stronger because of this. So when others aim low in your direction, rise above their jealousy and negativity, high enough to where they will never be able to reach you because anyone who prefers to focus on your lows instead of your peaks has no place in your life.

exit to the left.

What are you running from? What truth lies
beneath the spine of your book? What have you been
concealing with that smile? Where do you go when
you need to go so far that you can get away from
the pain and the struggle of realizing that none of
this will ever be easy to escape? The darkness drapes
itself over your heart and you can't help but crave
a light that'll show you the way toward something
better. Your feet are tired from walking in circles of
hope invested in people filled with the wrong type
of energy. People who say just enough to make you
stay, just enough to make you feel like walking away
will somehow push you further into the darkness
even though you've already experienced the worst
part. What are you running from? Who are you
trying to escape? Where do you go when going away
is possibly the only thing you have left?

weak men cheat
weak men lie
weak men make no effort
weak men cause confusion
weak men deserve none of you
or anything you have to offer
weak men will read this
and be offended
weak men will read this
and never change
stay away from weak men
do not waste your strength
on a man too weak to love you

she felt like feeling nothing
she just wants to forget
she just wants to free herself
she's just tired of regret

she is you
and she is ready
she's been searching
for something more
she is ready to move on
she's closer to the door

she listened with ears
like wolves
unafraid of the sound
of the footsteps
from those who would come
to try and break her down

---

i hope you find someone who hates
hurting your heart

hot like tea in the morning
soothing like whiskey
on a chilly afternoon

she is that and i love it

her silence was loud
you could hear everything
she wasn't saying
you could see the words
in her eyes
she spelled it all out
with a look

the tears will flow heavily
as if almost to drown you

the sadness will overrun
your soul
and take captive of your mind

there will be moments
where you feel like quitting
there will be days
where it all feels like too much

there will be nights
where sleep will escape you
and waking up the next morning
will be the hardest thing
you'll ever have to do

but no matter what storm may come
you will always survive
because you are more powerful
than anything that arrives to break you

if all you ever have is yourself
then you
will save you
and that, in fact,
is enough

scene forty-four.

There's a lot going on with you, so much has changed
this year and yet so much of it feels the same. You
made promises to yourself that have gotten harder
to keep. You've been going through so much but
you've held it all together and in this very moment
you wonder how long you'll be able to withstand
all of the things that stand in your way of peace. I
can't begin to fully understand what you're truly
going through, I won't pretend to comprehend all
of your daily struggles but I can tell you this. There
is beauty waiting behind the curtain. There is an
honest assortment of peacefulness living beyond the
barriers and there is happiness awaiting you after
the storm. Just a little bit longer now and you'll be
where you're supposed to be and you'll feel what you
deserve to feel. Please, hold on.

there is something beautiful
that lives in the heart
of the girl with the broken smile
there is something beautiful
living inside
of the woman who seems broken
and i just want to find it
i just want to find her truth

———————————

there is something about you
that most people will never appreciate
but you must learn to love yourself
even when others can't

you don't belong to him
no man can own the moon

guard your candle
not everyone you meet
deserves your light

the way women
can withstand
several storms
all at once
is something
to be inspired by

scene forty-five.

You're always giving but who gives to you? You're
always fighting for someone but who fights for you?
How is it that you've gone so long constantly trying
for someone who refuses to try just as much as you
do? Who taught you to settle? Was it a parent? Was
it your father or mother? You learned to tolerate
bullshit so young and so you grow older to seek after
more of that. Entertaining relationships that come
with dead ends. Falling in love with people who will
never catch you. It's time for you to be the recipient
of everything you've wasted on people who could
never live up to the things they promised. It's your
turn to know how it feels to be with someone who
would do anything to keep you.

scene forty-six.

None of it makes sense, none of this adds up. You're
unsure because they're uncertain. You're confused
because they seem to be unsure about you and you
choose to do more of what seems to not be working.
You decide to give more even though you know
you shouldn't. Maybe your heart is too big to just
throw in the towel. Maybe your soul feels like it'll
be giving up too much, even though you've already
given up way too much of yourself. It's possible that
their confusion has fooled you into believing that
someday they'll change but maybe the love you
deserve is just something they were never willing to
give you. Maybe this was all a lie from the beginning.
A lie that you chose to believe in because it
resembled everything you never had before. I think
your family set you up. I think your father failed you
or maybe your mother did. Maybe you're lacking this
ability to believe that you deserve more than you've
settled for because your parents failed at teaching
you self-confidence, self-awareness, love and peace.
It's possible that you missed that lesson on what love
actually was and so you've found yourself on a path
that leads to everything it isn't.

Listen to what I'm saying. Use your eyes like ears to hear this truthful melody. Consume every word as if it were food for your soul or a life force for your heart. Understand each word like your life depended on it because your life does depend on your ability to walk away from people who refuse to give you reasons to stay. You may not have gotten the proper education in terms of love and it's true meaning but I believe that you are smart enough and strong enough to survive the aftermath of leaving behind the people you believed loved you. I believe in your ability to let go just as you've believed in their lies long enough to hold on. None of it makes sense, none of it adds up. The love they claim to have for you just makes you feel empty and maybe it's time for you to fill yourself up with your own love. Maybe it's time for you to walk away just to get closer to yourself. You have to know that you mean something, you have to realize that something good is waiting for you behind all the people who have chosen to waste your time but you just have to learn to look past them in order to see more of what you truly deserve.

scene forty-seven.

You're strong and this has meant that you are always
there for others but no one is truly there for you in
the ways that you've made yourself available to them.
You don't even take it personal, you've learned how
to navigate through the issues that have plagued
your life on your own. You don't really seek the same
type of attention from others because you're not even
sure if anyone could even do what you do because,
in fact, not everyone has a heart the size of yours.
Not everyone is as selfless as you are, not everyone
holds this ability to care for others even when others
are rarely there to care for them and just like you, I
relate. My own words resonate deeply with the both
of us, you and I. This is how I know that you're not
truly alone because I feel the same way as you do.

I feel it even more when the days get longer and the
night is too uncomfortable for sleep. I feel it as well
when the heart wants someone to care for it but the
mind understands and registers the fact that most
people don't give a fuck or they don't care as much
as you do . . . as much as we do but I won't lose hope
for you. I won't lose hope for us. I still believe that

there is someone who will match your ability to care for them. I still believe that there is someone who will be present every time you need them but most importantly, I still and will always believe in you.

scene forty-eight.

people rarely hear you
you're so used to being ignored.
neglected, disrespected
and overlooked entirely

there's this weariness
in your eyes and it shows
whenever you stare off
into the night sky
trying to withstand it all
refusing to fall
even as your knees
give way to loads of heartache

you press on and press forward
without taking a break
running along the lines of giving in
without taking a breath

how much longer can you survive
how much further will you go

these questions tap dance

on your mind's floor
your brain feels it
like a blow to the head
but this blow to your heart
can render all hope dead

you say things with your silence
but people rarely comprehend it
you're so used to being ignored
and so you say nothing
in hopes of avoiding the disappointment
that still comes for you
like the flu during the winter

there are scars, so many scars
seemingly sketched across your skin
scars like painful stories
that you avoid telling
in hopes of appearing fine
but your eyes are saying
something different
your eyes are shouting something
and most people don't know

what you're saying or what it means

you move forward
as if that is the only direction to go
you move forward
when most individuals would stop moving
at all and at most, all hope has been lost
but you carry on anyway

they rarely hear you
they rarely care
but you never give up
and that itself
is the most powerful thing
you could ever do

dear you, this moment.

I am writing this from my office, perched high above the Manhattan streets. It's a Sunday evening and the sky is lit a pale blue hue of calm and quietness. It's much more melodic than it was earlier today. The sirens, the stomping of the feet and the sound of cars screeching and screaming was dreadfully out of place as this city was in a rage between the hours of noon and half past three. I am writing this purely out of this random thought that I had about you. Yes you, the aching soul that has been reading these words. Your fingers resting on this page. Your heavy heart weighing you down into a pit of despair. In this moment I care, maybe more than I should. You and I, strangers, familiar with the same chaos that plagues the heart of someone willing to love people who are incapable of loving us back. The both of us strangers but drawn together in this moment like rain water to roses. The sky is a bit darker now, the streets below a bit quieter and I can't help but think you're reading these words in a room beside a sky that is similar to my own. Regardless of who you are, where you are, and what you're feeling. In this moment, you're not alone because I'm here, within these words. I'm here and I hope that helps and if it doesn't, I believe that you will find the comfort you need, I believe that you will discover that very thing that you desire most. Whatever it is, wherever you are.

Sincerely,
Sin

new way of thinking.

Let's create new ideas, new ways of thinking. New ways of approaching life and relationships. Can we stop encouraging women to stay with mates who aren't worthy of their affection? Those lists in magazines that give women tips on how to maintain relationships should actually be teaching women how to let go of one that no longer makes them happy. Do these publications even realize that by providing tips in every issue for women to follow, that they're actually making the woman out to be the issue when she really isn't? How can these women, my sisters, my readers, my supporters, ever begin to move on toward what will help them find peace if all they're ever encouraged to do is stay and fight and try for someone who treats their relationship like a story with no meaning?

Let's create new ways of thinking, new ways of approaching good relationships and unhealthy ones. Let's explore this idea that self-love is a love that is worth chasing after and that true romance begins with self. Let us encourage women to seek more of themselves and to only entertain a relationship with someone who encourages harmony and peace. It's hard for so many women to walk away because their minds have been flooded with ideas on how to continue showing up in relationships that feel more like prison sentences. I guess I've been hoping for some sort of change in the exchange of knowledge and ideas on a global scale but that hasn't happened. This is why I wrote this and this is why I'm here speaking to you.

I know love has felt unkind but the truth is, the love you've come to know has never been anything more than a distraction or a wall, keeping you from seeing the real thing. I know relationships have been difficult, they weigh heavily on your heart as you struggle to move forward but those relationships were more like a version of hell that you didn't deserve. I hope you read these words and discover a new way of thinking, a new way of approaching this idea of finding the proper mate and I want you to know that in order to do so, you have to find yourself again. You have to remember your own strength and you have to realize that a relationship doesn't define you. Your value depends strictly on yourself and who you are as an individual, especially while single. You don't have to rush yourself into anything that isn't making you smile or encouraging you to feel a peace of mind, always. Who you are is not to be wrapped up into who is pursuing you. It's not your job to keep anyone but yourself. Don't be so hard on your own heart. Don't be so distracted by this need to be with someone that you forget about yourself and all the things you deserve. Let's create a new way of thinking, a new idea of a love that doesn't have to hurt.

midnight.

My heart is probably the same shade as the moon
tonight. Bleak and pale, almost empty of any hue
that would suggest some sort of joy. I've been
sipping on the same coffee for the last few hours,
overwhelmed by sadness and yet underwhelmed
by you. Who are you exactly? You are the nothing
that I forced into something. A someone who made
me feel like a nobody. You wrapped your pretty lies
with enough words to sound like truth, telling me
everything I wanted to hear. Whispering like the
devil while wearing white like angels. Your words
were comforting at first but they feel deadlier than
ever as I sit here beside the window, re-reading
your texts, playing back everything that happened
the night before. How did we even get here? How
did I let this happen? I lost myself! Where have I
gone? And why did it end? What was I thinking?
Maybe I wasn't. My mind went blind at the sight of
you and my brain surrendered its power of choice
to my heart. Of course, I get it now. That's where I
went wrong. Ignoring what I thought and leaving it
to fade away in the shadow of what I felt. My heart
betrayed me the moment it chose you but I had no

idea at that time but now here we are, or honestly, here I am. Alone and aching beneath the weight of all the empty promises and emotional dead ends. My heart seems to have led me into a lion's den or maybe this is a killing field and you are like the vultures, flying above my head. Waiting to pick at me.

This isn't the first time we've ended up in a place like this but something tells me that this will surely be the last. I thought my heart couldn't take any more bad news but it's not like I was given a choice and you most likely no longer care about breaking me down any further. I shouldn't be surprised but I am. I guess it's hard to prepare for an end that arrives so sudden. I think it's difficult to prepare for a death when there are moments where you feel so alive with the person you've fought so hard to keep. Sometimes I think you were never really mine to begin with. I feel like this was more of a dream that spoiled into a nightmare but at the same time I feel awake with my eyes closed.

With an open heart, you tend to see what you want and despite all of the shit you put me through, all I ever saw was us and all I ever wanted were the things you promised me, after apologizing for doing the things you refused to stop doing. All I ever wanted was a truth you weren't capable of telling and a love that you were never ready to provide. I get it now but I've come to these realizations a moment too late to spare myself from falling over into a pit of my own despair. I completely understand but that doesn't make it hurt any less than it has. I believe I saw it coming but I decided to pay more attention to the good even though the bad was a major component in our relationship.

It always starts off the same, you know? Every relationship begins with this overall phase of bliss, trust and dependency. There are more laughs in the beginning. It's almost as if everything is a bit funnier toward the front end of the courtship. You find yourself smiling for no damn reason and as foolish as you may look to others, you don't care because you've found something worth looking foolish over.

That was me at one point, that was us, do you remember? You belonged to someone else and I felt like I won because you chose me. I mean I feel much different about that now as I reflect on the past and how we came together. I now understand that the way we fell into each other's lives would also be the way we left . . . you left.

The last weeks of our impending doom did not reflect the first weeks of our affair. Leaving what you believed was love is an entirely different experience than walking toward it and I can honestly say that who I am in this moment wouldn't even recognize the person I was when you decided to walk out on your ex for me. Going back to that feeling of being chosen by you, the dopamine that surged throughout my body whenever my phone rang or notified me of your text. I'll say it without shame, the decision to be with me over whomever you were with before me fed my ego. The loneliness that existed in my life before you made me eager to accept your advances and I did.

Sometimes I wish I never allowed you to hide me until you were ready to claim me in the open, to the public. Sometimes I wish my self-esteem was a bit higher or that I loved myself a bit more than I did back then. I think that's what I was lacking, that ability to care for myself in a way that would keep me from compromising my mind and body for a relationship that would prove unworthy of my effort. If I would have cared about myself fully, I wouldn't have sought out a love that you could never actually give me but this is what happened and this is where we are. It's midnight and my heart is probably the same shade as the moon tonight. Bleak and pale, nearly empty of any hue that would suggest that I even know what true happiness is. Bleak and empty, without any color and all that is left is this newfound darkness that currently complicates my existence. All that remains is the nothing you left me with but for some odd reason, I know that I'll survive this.

process, letting go.

Let go of him by loving yourself more than he's chosen to. Let go of him by realizing that you are worth more than he can ever comprehend. I guess I'm just hoping that these words will make a difference. Maybe they won't, maybe they will . . . no matter what I'll keep trying. Let go of him because the love you claim to have for him causes you pain. Let go of him by choosing happiness over pain and heartache. When you love yourself, giving yourself to the wrong person is something you'll try your hardest to avoid. Let go of him and keep yourself!

hell settle.

I just hope you stop giving your time, energy, and love to someone who is committed only to their desire to hurt you. Hard to believe in a love that feels like joy when you've settled for a love that resembles hell.

there's just something about you
that most people will never get
your existence is written in a language
that most of them will never comprehend

you're a moment, you're this memory
you're an unforgettable event
proof of angels living on earth
you've always been heaven sent

goals for this year: survive, again.

who will you become when you refuse to settle for
less than you deserve

———————————

she emerged from the darkness
like a wolf filled with lightning

the energy you wasted
on trying harder for him

give it to yourself

i swear to you
women like her
lit the moon

don't complain about her
being cold
knowing damn well
she wasted her warmth on you

take the pen from his hands
and write your own ending
he no longer fits
in your story

she is king
she could rule
without him

she was more than enough
but you lost her

---

it's hard to fit women like you into a poem but i try

---

it was midnight and no matter how dark it became
she found ways to produce her own light

she ran barefoot through the fiery chaos
without fear because flames can't stop
the woman who is used to surviving

there is a power swelling beneath your skin
inside your bones
unleash it

women are the fingerprint of strength

the woman you ignored
became my favorite melody
and I'd do anything
to hear her song

don't forget to love yourself
a little·harder today, tonight
always

scene forty-nine.

The first man she'd ever love was the first man she'd
be disappointed by. His best example of what a man
was would later lead her into the arms of the worst
men she could ever choose and this is why I don't
blame her for choosing the type of guy whom she
could never truly depend on. Her first love was her
father, he taught her to settle because in order to love
him, she had to put aside his worst traits. She had
to ignore all of his flaws. She took a cracked canvas
and painted over it in an attempt to make something
beautiful. She took what little he gave her and did
what she could to make it appear more than what it
truly was. He taught her how to love a man and so
she went on to care for men who lacked the same
things her father did.

she's a wolf
but even wolves feel pain

---

i don't want to say i suffer from depression
i thrive through it

---

all of my critics are underachievers

---

aren't you tired of drowning, reaching up for the
person who is too weak, too selfish to care

hell is looking over
at the person you love
and realizing that they hate
to see you happy

don't let old flames
distract you from a new fire
worth burning bright

she herself was a sword
and she'd cut her enemies deep
by simply existing

whatever he denied her of
she decided to give to herself

she knew love was a night sky
because all her life
the stars would fall for her

she held her own hand
she led herself toward
the love she felt she deserved

---

her rose had more thorns
than the rest
and yet she bloomed beautifully

rebel against this idea
of letting him hurt your heart

rebel against the pain
he wants you to feel

make him irrelevant
by remembering that he is not a prize
and that you were always worth
fighting for

she's worth everything
i knew this the moment
i heard her laugh

it hurts in the beginning
but the end was necessary
and one day you'll realize
that you'll be everything
to the right person

until then
be everything to yourself

in love:22

what you did
and who you were
has nothing to do
with what you mean
to me now

who you were before me
will never stop me from loving
the person you've evolved into

you are not your mistakes
you are not the brokenness
you've felt

you are more than a girl
who knew nothing but pain
you are that someone
who saved me

we fell into heaven
hand in hand
heart to heart
your soul with mine

in love 2/22.

you and your OCD
me and my overthinking
and yet there are moments
when our only obsession
is making each other smile

sometimes when we're together
we forget about those mental battles
those wars seem to take a backseat
whenever i'm sitting beside you

in love 2:22.

what i love about you
is the way your smile
dances like stars
under a midnight moon

all in all
you deserve someone
who you can be vulnerable with
and not worry about
being hurt because of it

a life.

Life doesn't have to be so damn complicated. I think it's important to find a flow that works for you and encourages a stable mental health. A flow that brings you joy and peace. Building a life that represents everything you think you deserve with people who deserve to be a part of your life. That's the biggest thing, being careful about whom or what you give your energy to.

give me friendship
tell me the truth always
try to understand me
especially when i open up
and let's communicate more

give me the freedom
of being able to trust you
without doubt
and i will love you
for life

in you lives
a version of beauty
too profound for words

and it doesn't matter
who sees it in you
as long as you
see it within yourself

scene fifty.

she sat there
on the edge
of letting go
unafraid of leaping
away from everything
that caused her sadness

she sat there
on the edge
of everything
that no longer
deserved her energy

she sat there
on the edge
of moving on
and rediscovering
everything she lost
while loving
the wrong person

she sat there
on the edge
ready to leap
toward herself

scene fifty-one.

i've been hoping
that you weren't too hurt
to pick yourself up

i sit here hoping
that you haven't forgotten
your true worth

i'm here writing this
to you in hopes
that it will reach you in time
because my heart seems
to have made an investment
in someone i don't even know

and deep down i simply hope
that you'll read this
and realize that you are better
without the people who hurt you

a moonlit room.

Sometimes she wishes she'd never met him. Those regrets linger in her soul like darkness during midnight. She's at war with her own heart, struggling with the idea of him and the truth of his actions. He was always good at saying all the right things, he spoke of his intentions as if he was sure he'd follow through but the moment she let him in, he once more reminded her of why she'd always feared allowing someone close to her heart in the first place. In the beginning she was hopeful, similar to any start. Not knowing that this particular ending would eventually tear her apart.

Too many endings.

You became distant all of a sudden and my heart
felt so heavy in that moment of realizing that maybe
we wouldn't last, crashed into an ending that would
send me into the darkest abyss. Struggling to find
sleep while it is you that I miss. We had bliss, we had
joy, we had peace and so much hope. Now I sit here
clueless with a look that screams, "I don't know."

Too many endings, where should I begin? Losing
my mind, oftentimes my soul drifts in the wind. This
ache breaks the glass ceiling above my head as all of
my dreams come crashing down upon me. We ended
and I'm pretending.

the rain whispers your name
the moon is so inviting
you feel like the night
twisted and dark but beautiful

---

she is evolving into the woman
you will never deserve

she transformed into everything
you could never comprehend

she's learning to leap above heartache
she's learning to rise above the chaos
of a broken heart

she is you
a maddening light
that refuses to compromise
the magic that dwells within

you are becoming more
evolving into something greater

you are what happens
when a rose finds the perfect light

you bloom for yourself

16h.

Women don't have to be in a relationship to feel like a Queen. I believe that a woman has the ability to crown herself. To hold herself when others refuse to. Choosing herself when others don't. Loving herself when others are incapable.

24h.

Stop trying for someone who refuses to make an effort to help you achieve a peace of mind.

Stop letting your ex distract you from being happy without them.

our stories, our pain.

Tomorrow didn't come, forever was too short. I still remember the sound of my heart banging against a wall filled with every promise you made, each word painting a visual of what your lies looked like. Imagine playing back everything you thought was true, only to discover the deception after you had given everything to the one person who deserved nothing.

I think you know exactly what I'm talking about, you've felt the shards of sharp pieces of your heart in the palm of your hands as you tried to piece yourself back together. I know your pain and you know mine and so here we are, meeting here on these pages. I want to forget and so do you. I want to remember how it felt to be happy and so do you.

self, start there.

I learned a long time ago that real love begins from
within. I think my love-for-self brought me the type
of relationship that resembled everything I knew I
wanted and deserved. Time alone after an unhealthy
relationship helped me rediscover my own self-
worth. Doing more of what I loved or spending
more time on myself helped me focus in on my
strengths, the things I admire about myself and so
much more. It also gave me a moment to self-reflect
on what I should do to better myself. I think self-
love is wrapped up in how we choose to evolve. I
think self-love can be cultivated by simply chasing
this portion of peace. A happier me meant a happier
life and living good attached to the right mate. When
you don't love yourself, you're more likely to love a
person who chooses to hurt you. When you don't
love yourself, it's hard to accept real love from the
right person. I think we must do the work, we must
focus on ourselves before we can ever understand or
be prepared to focus on someone else. The love feels
so pure when you take time to understand it outside
of a relationship.

you are not fabric
do not let him try you on

wake up, please.

Someone told you as a little girl that when a guy
is mean to you, he likes you and so you grew up
thinking that their mistreatment was a confession
of love when honestly it was a red flag for the pain
they'd cause.

Maybe the good are invisible to you because they
taught you that the bad boys were more interesting
and yet interestingly enough, the bad boys are the
reason for your heartache and the destruction of
your peace.

done all you can.

You're this wonderful representation of love. Sure, you're imperfect but you try your hardest for the ones you care about. Your kind heart has become familiar with heartache as you often find yourself struggling with the idea of starting over without the person you thought you needed. Things go wrong even as you try your hardest to keep it together and yet somehow you feel guilty for doing nothing more than simply demanding what you deserve. It hurts my heart to know that the woman reading this book has somehow gotten to the point where she thinks it's all her fault and so she willingly puts up with the b.s. from the one person who no longer deserves her energy. You take them back because for some odd reason you've grown accustomed to the pain and disappointment and it hurts your soul because you've done all you can to prove that you're worthy of someone who will never be worthy of you. I'll be honest, even though you sometimes feel broken, even though you sometimes feel like a mess, you are allowed to be imperfect. You are allowed to be demanding. You are allowed to be upset. No one is allowed to make you feel bad for simply loving and wanting to be loved. No one is allowed to take advantage of your kindness. Don't let the person who will never live up to the standards of love that you deserve somehow make you feel like it's your fault for giving a damn about them. Don't let that person make you feel like it's your fault that things aren't working out. Stop trying to keep a person who doesn't deserve to stay. Stop fighting for someone who is too weak to fight for you and the relationship. Too often, the heart of a powerful woman falls into the hands of someone who is too much of a coward to even appreciate the woman who loves them. It's not your fault that they could never live up to what they promised. Maybe this helps, maybe it won't, but still, I'm not giving up on you.

deep down, you.

Now what was I saying? Oh yeah, that's it. It's time
to level on anyone who has treated you like shit. It's
been too long, constantly feeling like you're not good
enough for someone who refuses to be good to you.
It's time to be good to yourself. I know you've been
reaching out to them for help but they're not even
trying. You've been drowning, nearly dying, but you
must save yourself. You must remain defiant because
deep down, even though it may not feel like it, you
have the heart and the pride of several lions.

you are a golden moon
in a darkened sky
you are the light that lives
without the presence of the sun

all powerful
truly divine

midnight would mean nothing
without you

the problem was
you were trying to create
a good love
with someone who
was bad for your heart

and love can't grow
without care on both ends

enCOURAGE.

Let's encourage women to be brave enough to walk away instead of placing heavy blame or making them feel guilty for giving up on someone who quit on them a long time ago.

dear woman, your nature is brilliant
your existence inspires the sun
to rise

the ones we miss.

I miss you, I thought this would be easy but it isn't
and the hardest part of it all is that you don't even
give a damn about me. You left when I needed you
the most, you disappeared on me when the sadness
came for me and there was nothing I could do but sit
up in the dark, looking toward the moon for clarity.
Struggling to find my peace of mind in the dark
hues of the night. If you loved me like you claimed,
you'd be here. If I was the one, I'd never feel like the
nothing I've felt while being near you. I miss you, I
miss me. I lost you and lost myself.

guilty men shake
full of fear
in the presence
of my words

guilty men
feel threatened and attacked
when i inform women
and encourage women, good

you left
now do this heart a favor
and don't look this way
when you wish to return
because this heart
is no longer open to you

Don't focus so much on being in a relationship. Focus more on being happy and understand that happiness can be achieved by yourself. The joy that is cultivated from within will bring you everything your heart desires. We're so focused on getting all the things of the world and living by a certain standard that we've forgotten to pursue ourselves and what truly makes us happy.

my mind has seen its worst days
it's been broken in several ways
and sometimes
i feel like i have yet to find
all of its pieces

real love would never make you
compromise your mental comfort zones
and that's the battle

finding someone who cares
about the condition of your mind
your heart, body and soul

be careful who
you give your
midnights to

still here.

It bothers me because you don't even know who you are anymore. You let him run wild with no restraint, all throughout your heart and mind. He's the reason you're not sleeping tonight and it bothers me to have to sit here and write this in hopes that it'll reach you in time. It feels like we're running out of time or maybe I'm overreacting to you acting like you don't give a fuck when obviously this guy has wrecked your heart so often that you allow it because you're used to it. Saying you'll leave but you don't do it and I guess that bothers me. This idea of you hiding from what's really happening in your soul, you feel so many things and yet you say nothing. You want so many things and yet you go without. You're tough like a pack of wolves but even wolves feel pain and I just wish you'd let it out because maybe that would make it easier to kick him out of your heart.

It bothers me because you don't even realize the power that you have and I wish you'd take ownership over your future by leaving him behind in your past. He belongs with everything that barely fits in your rearview mirror. He belongs anywhere farthest from you and it bothers me that you'll read this and possibly let him back in where he'll never truly fit. You're forcing a narrative that could never end well and I just want you to be happy. What truly bothers me is that you're reading this book, relating to all these words when honestly, I wish this didn't resonate with you. Regardless of what you decide, I'll be here.

void of peace.

Loving the wrong person is like a nightmare that
feels impossible to wake up from but you can't
continue to compromise your dreams for something
that no longer fits into the idea of what you believe
you deserve.

1/8/13.

If your loyalty isn't appreciated, it's okay to walk away. Loving someone means remaining by their side but there's only so much you can do with someone who isn't mature enough to understand your true value.

5/8/13.

Stop sacrificing yourself and your happiness for a love that requires you to feel pain.

7/13/13.

Most times when a woman has been hurt in the past, everything becomes transparent. She sees with a new version of clarity. She's heard it all before, she's lived it more than once. You can attempt to lie to her but she'll always discover the truth.

8/8/13.

A woman's pain tolerance is unmatched, her patience is legendary. She loves hard and her loyalty is remarkable.

Appreciate her more . . .
Love and devote yourself to her more . . .

do not stay
where your heart
can't grow

never allow your loyalty
to become a form of slavery

her choice.

Maybe she's single by choice. Maybe she's decided that after some time of being overlooked, underappreciated and neglected that she no longer wants to be placed in a situation where she feels like she's wasting her time. Maybe she's single because she promised herself to never settle for less than what she's always wanted and deserves.

8/30/13.

she won't give up on you easily
but that doesn't mean
you should see how far
you can go with causing her pain
before she's finally gone

never rely on your tongue
when your soul is tired
and your heart is angry

you end up saying hurtful things
that you never really meant

10/23/13.

Never take a woman's trust for granted. You'll never truly understand how difficult it may have been for her to invest trust in you, knowing that everyone she's ever trusted failed her at one time or another.

someone attentive
someone devoted

10/31/13.

One day, you'll see. One day those apologies will
hold no meaning, she'll no longer provide you with
a second chance to hurt her heart and she'll give you
nothing but silence because you will have lost the
right to hear her speak. Every woman has a breaking
point, every woman experiences that moment
from which they believe walking away and finding
themselves is the true reward.

11/9/13.

If he no longer appreciated your presence, then maybe he'll comprehend your absence. Stop making time for someone who refuses to find time for you.

11/11/13.

I wish he understood that every time he takes you for granted, he's just teaching you how to live without him.

———————————

men play themselves whenever
they're unfaithful to good women

12/3/13.

Every woman has a breaking point that causes apologies to be deemed useless, a point where "love" no longer carries weight or meaning. What I'm trying to say is that it doesn't matter how much she loves you, if you push her to that point, she'll make up her mind to walk away.

the drama is unattractive
and completely underwhelming

key stroke 2014.

missing your words
i find peace in each letter
you type

i find inspiration in each
emotion you share
i fall in love with every keystroke
cloud nine in the moments
you press send, sending me
all that is within you

everything that completely relates
to all that lives within me
i've fallen for the words
of your heart
and the sentences of your soul

i crave only you

Tuesday, 4/8/14.

i'd dive deeper
to your ocean's floor
in an attempt to explore
overflowing with anticipation
always eager to discover more

i'd drown a thousand times
if it meant touching your core
craving more of your depth
you've been all
that i've been searching for

our kisses caused a rapture
an overflowing surge of vibration
knees weak, heavy hearted
we fell in lust

kisses.

i miss you
almost like the desert
misses the rain

often overthinking
i wonder if you've ever
felt the same
while alone in your space

am i the one
you think about
you won't say it
with your mouth
but your mind
is calling out

i miss you
this shit is real
i hope you feel it

i miss you most nights
and that's just something
i'll have to deal with

a text i never sent.

The first thing on my mind, you live here with permission to stay as long as you please. So please walk freely, run if you'd like to, I don't care as long as you do it within me, within my mind.

why he hides you.

Oh my generation, filled with so many lost souls.
Easily influenced by the songs they hear and the
movies they watch. Being taught about love from
people who don't love them. Entering relationships
that are more like a personal hell, remaining in a
relationship that causes their heart to go up into
flames. I see so many women enter relationships
with men who aren't men enough to celebrate them
but instead, they simply hide them in plain sight. If
for some reason you are the woman who is tired of
being hidden or kept a secret, read on . . .

I won't waste your time, I won't dance around the
obvious truth. I'll instead, simply spell it out for
you with as much detail as I can. He hides you
because he'd much rather appear available when
in all honesty, he's technically taken by you. He's
not fully invested and it becomes apparent by his
refusal to showcase his appreciation for you. It's the
same old bullshit. They'll hit you with the being
private conversation and how much they value their
privacy as they continuously post some of the most
private and sentimental moments in their lives via

social media while conveniently leaving you out of the picture as if you don't even exist. Now if you're the woman who tells people that it's just I.G. or it's just social media and that you don't care that you're not important enough to be shared on his timeline, then these words aren't for you. I'm only talking to the women who are tired of being treated as if they don't matter. I'm only speaking to the women who are tired of being left out of picture . . . literally. I honestly think it's sad that men have this ability to manipulate and change the narrative of what a woman wants by making her feel as if she's asking for too much. So, I know that there will be some women who read this, pretending that they don't care, as if that makes them appear to be strong or secure but in all honesty, it doesn't. It actually hurts me to see or know that you've found yourself in a relationship with someone who would rather treat you like they're embarrassed to be with you.

Privacy has nothing to do with keeping someone hidden. Sharing your love for someone, whether it be in a caption or a photo, doesn't disrupt privacy and in a world where people share the most important things in their lives with the whole world via social media, how is it that you've accepted being left out or made to look like a ghost to their present lives? A man who hides you is hiding something that'll eventually break your heart. Think about it . . .

she was saving herself.

It was almost as if her sun no longer wanted to
rise and her moon began to lose its glow. She was
powerful but she was tired. She was in love but at
the same time, she was in hell. Stuck in this loop
of wanting to move on but struggling to let go
and her heart was too heavy to carry on her own,
yet somehow she did. Somehow she kept going
when giving up felt like the only option. She began
choosing herself in a way that no one else could
and instead of continuing to fall, she'd found herself
rising to new heights. Above the pain she felt, above
the drama that had plagued her life. She renewed her
own journey, she saved her own soul.

_____

compose your own melody
create your own song

i'm just not the person

you hurt anymore

you are no longer my moon
i found a way to change my stars

she's evolving beyond
everything that used to
break her

your heart is not theirs
to break

you belong to you
and your heart is yours
not theirs

she made pain look beautiful
the way she survived
the way she chose to move forward
even when giving up
felt like the best option

maybe you're the strong one
maybe you've held on
because you're strong enough
to love unconditionally
but maybe it's time
to use your strength
to move forward
with your life

soul relatable II.

I think it's important for you to know that it's okay
to be on your own, be single. There is nothing
wrong with being by yourself for awhile. Do what
makes you happy even if it means walking away
from someone who failed to act on their own
potential of being a good partner to you. Destroy
the cycle of going back to things that only provide
you with reasons to walk away. You can't pursue
happiness while chasing down people who make you
miserable.

i found happiness
the day i found an exit
out of your life

burn bridges without regret
burn bridges for light
to see in darkness

burn bridges and use them
as torches to light the path
to something better

the pretending.

I used to wonder how someone with so many friends
could seem so sad. Social media pics of parties,
the imagery of loud music, drinking and then I got
to know who your friends were and realized that
instead of trying to help you cope with everything
that was going on, their entire focus was only to have
a good time at the expense of your desire to avoid
loneliness but even then, in a room filled with people
or a phone filled with contacts, you were always so
alone. I noticed that . . .

something to think about.

He was in love with the softness of your thighs and the build of your frame. He was in love with the possibilities of getting what he wanted. He was in love with the wetness of the inside of your mouth. He was in love with it, not you and that's the entire truth. So, don't tell me you've been in love when he provided nothing but lists for you to fall into. Love doesn't neglect the soul or disrespect the mind or fail to protect the heart. True love doesn't walk away whenever you say no or cause you to compromise your happiness. You keep saying you've been in love, well where is he now? Where is this love you claim while questioning the way he feels about you? Real love is certain and always sure. I just hope you'd realize this.

3:33am
3:33am

3:33am
3:33am

3:33am

3:33am

3:33am

4/19/15 I.

The longer you stay in a relationship with someone
who refuses to love you, the more you shorten
the length of the future you'd otherwise spend
with your soulmate. How much time do you have
left to waste? How long are you willing to be in
a relationship with someone other than your
soulmate? Life is too short. We always think we
have so much time until it's too late.

4/19/15 II.

Doesn't it get tiring to smile when you're unhappy?
You have found yourself falling for someone who
was great at first but that image slowly faded and
now you feel stuck because the person you love no
longer exists but physically he's there, so you're left
holding on to someone that feels empty, something
that drains your heart. Someone who now causes
you to feel empty as well. You're not stupid, you're
human and instead of beating down your own
heart for loving the wrong person, look at it like
this, at least you're strong enough to give your love
to someone. In time, I hope you find the strength to
let go.

you know what
i stopped trying
to resurrect
what we had
and began to plan
the funeral

i found happiness
after i realized
that losing you
would never be
a loss

her broken heart was the gift
he would never deserve

he hit her with words
and even if the bruises
on her heart began to fade
the pain was still there

there are moments
when change
can be painful
but what hurts
the most

is being stuck in places
where you no longer
desire to roam

she screamed pain
with silence
she wore heartache
with a smile

Plath, Monroe.

Plath went down
a haunting path
and my words
were too late
to reach her

there are many things
I would've told Monroe
and it hurts to think
that these words
could have saved
her soul

but maybe this book
will reach you
in time

now and then.

maybe my love
was far too big
a picture

to fit into
the frame
of your life

maybe my moon
was too bright
for your nights

and maybe the words
in my book
were far too complex
for you to comprehend

i know that now
i wish i knew
that
then

how strange it is
that you can be brought
to life with the first kiss
and destroyed
by the last

first love
doesn't mean
a lasting love

she outgrew
the person she was
in exchange for the one
she was always supposed to be

stop forcing life
into the ghost
of everything
he used to be

our end
was the beginning
of something better
with myself

Sunday, someday.

You knew all along, you were just too afraid to accept it. Something changed and the person you thought you knew now felt unfamiliar. Maybe it was their tone of treatment, no longer soft and loving. Maybe it was the fact that you could no longer depend on them to show up whenever you needed them. The mind always knows, even while the heart takes longer to process the truth, but you knew. You always knew.

_____

she loved who she thought he was

imagine a place
where he can't hurt you

now go there

done, emotionally.

She hid you in her tears for so long. All the pain you caused, the lies you told, hidden away. Locked up inside. One day she began to weep, she had finally broken down from this weight that she'd been carrying and every tear contained a memory, a piece of you as she was literally purging away all the times you caused her heart to feel miserable.

She cried because she was finished.

She cried because she was done being hurt by you.

these wars.

Part of the battle has always been trying to separate
the heart from the hands of someone who no longer
deserves the opportunity to hold it. The journey
toward everything you once were is often the hardest
path to follow. There's this fading memory of the
person you used to be before you met them. There's
this translucent figure of everything you wanted to
be before they entered your life. You never notice
it in the beginning but the moment you fell for
them, you lost the biggest part of everything you
were destined to become and everything you were
destined to have gets replaced with all the things you
thought you needed. You soon enough discover that
the love of your life becomes the hell in your life and
thus, the journey to walk away begins.

1w I.

Self-love first. Everything begins with you. Peace and joy can both be obtained without a relationship. A relationship is supposed to enhance everything you've cultivated on your own.

lw II.

You are not obligated to stay where you are not appreciated. You are not obligated to consider someone who is inconsiderate when it comes to you. It may be hard to let go, it may be hard to move on but if you want to be happy, you'll need to love yourself more than you love someone who acts like they hate you.

lw III.

Deciding to find someone to love doesn't mean you have to lose yourself in the process. Loving the right person will never distract you from caring about yourself.

---

like the moon
hiding behind the sunlight
you've hidden your pain
behind a smile

he was never the stars
nor was he the moon
he was always the darkness
that kept you restless

---

how easy it is to become a poet
when your heart is flooded with pain
and misery

please don't let your dreams
of love die
behind the person
who doesn't deserve you

she has always been art
and her life is an exhibit
of strength and courage

this haunting idea.

It's terrifying. This thought of you giving all that you
have to someone who intends to give you nothing
is truly haunting and frustrating at times. I see
so much when I look at you and I'd hate for your
essence to be shared with someone who will only
cause you harm.

one hope.

You represent everything that someone has been searching their entire lives for. I hope you find the person who is searching for you.

still kind.

Your kindness is not a weakness, your ability to love is not a problem. Your heart has seen its fair share of disappointment and pain. Family, turning on you. Friends, toxic. Relationships that often fail to last but you must not let the sour souls of this earth spoil whatever good you have left within you. You must continue to evolve, even while others will claim you've changed as if there is something wrong with you for growing and wanting more out of life. You must not give them the power to dictate your future because honestly, anyone who wants to keep you back from becoming the person you're meant to be belongs in the past and you must figure out a way to properly leave them in your rearview mirror.

Do not let the sour souls of this earth use your kindness against you. There will be individuals who show up as distractions. Individuals who will only serve as a barrier between you and the life of love you deserve. Individuals who will only serve as lessons and examples of what not to want and who to avoid while continuing down this path called life. You must not allow them the power to keep you from the things you've been fighting for.

only fools tell writers what to write
only a fool would believe
that they could control
the writer's voice

they'll carry their opinions
they'll critique
while filled with rage
and frustration
because that fool
has no power
in the face
or in the presence
of a writer

my pen is a sword
too heavy
for you to hold
too powerful
for you to touch
too sharp
for you to dull

depression, new ideas.

What if this depression I feel is somehow a gift
wrapped in something society taught me to be afraid
of? What if this sadness is only a symbol of how
clearly I see the world and all its occupants? What
if this sadness is a symbol of how well adjusted I
am? I pose these lines as questions because it's more
relatable to ask questions than to make statements
that don't fit under the set standard of the world
we live in as if we're not allowed to think or see
things differently and so we hide our truths behind
hypotheticals. We've relied on the information of
others for so long that we've drowned out our own
facts and ideas. We're a collection of people who
have given strangers the power to define us against a
list of things that some of us were never meant to be,
keeping us from what we desire to become. Relying
on a diagnoses to better explain a truth that only we
ourselves are capable of understanding.

So, what's your prognosis, Doc? Is my ability to
feel the peaks of happiness or the lows of sadness
a problem? Or is it my gift, a gift you've denied so
many of by telling them they're sick when really
they're actually free.

heart inspire.

Throughout your entire life, you've faced the chaos alone. You've supplied yourself with everything needed to survive any oncoming storm. You stand among the heavy wind, beneath the piercing of the rain. You struggle at times but you still fight. You feel like quitting but you keep going. There's this undeniable source of power that dwells in your heart and you are truly the inspiration behind the words on these pages.

Thank you for lending your strength to this world. We need you. I need you.

bloom new meaning.

I keep dead roses on my table top in my office to
remind me that there is beauty in all things and
though these roses are dead, they seem to bloom
a new meaning. There is beauty in a sadness that
allows you to feel deeply, there is beauty in the end
because it gives way to a new beginning. There is
beauty in the broken because in crumbling beneath
emotion, there's this opportunity to be strengthened
by anything that has hurt you. This bundle of dead
roses may have lost its intrigue to most people but to
me, they inspire something beautiful. You may have
experienced your fair share of heartache, you know
what it means to feel empty or torn to pieces but I
assure you that there is still meaning living inside
your heart. There is still purpose and inspiration
dwelling within your soul.

introvert, new ideas.

Sometimes I feel like I'm sitting in a room without windows, the white walls almost appear to be padded and the silence plagues me like a calm and still storm. I should be afraid I guess, uncomfortable maybe but I am never more at peace than when sitting in the silence with nothing but the sound of my own heart. Being alone is not a punishment, it doesn't need to be. I'm more at home when alone or with my lover, away from people because the very thought of people drains me of my divine energy. I'm alone but not really because I'm well aware of the individuals who feel exactly like me. Maybe even you, we see seclusion and silence as a way to renew. A way to reboot. They judge us as if something is wrong, only because they misunderstand the melody in our song. The longing to get away and stay away in an attempt to find our way to a space where the meaningful happens. Labeling anti-everything when honestly we're only anti-things that have no purpose in our lives.

Sometimes I feel like I'm sitting in a room without windows, the white walls almost appear to be padded and while they wanted me to think I'm crazy for wanting to be by myself, maybe my sanity blooms insanely bright whenever I part ways with the chaos that is the world and the people I've decided to stay away from.

you are, you are III.

I have something to tell you
One more thing to say here
I have something I need you to know
Before I go
Before these words run out
Before this book ends

You have always meant the world to me
You were valuable before we even met
Before the words, before the books
Before you were my muse
You have always been everything
You are mighty, intelligent and significant
In case you forgot

There was a knock at the door . . .
Only it wasn't an actual door . . .
This was all a beautiful metaphor
To explain the way you entered my life
Through an open window
Via an inbox, my inbox

That night changed my life, Samantha

It was you who said "It's crazy how sometimes you have to be destroyed to be made anew" and it was me who said "Everything happens for a reason, just like this moment. I do believe that what you're dealing with will pass." In that moment and within that first conversation with you, it appeared to me that the pain had been so deep that you might have often felt like feeling nothing and so on that December night in 2014, you became the inspiration for "she felt like feeling nothing," there were so many things that I knew you'd wish you'd forget and move on from and on that December night in 2014, you became the inspiration for "she just wants to forget." You were that stranger, that woman, that weary soul, that aching heart that was strong but tired of dealing with versions of love that felt more like hatred. You became my whiskey, my words and a shovel, your love helped me bury the anguish and confusion I felt before I met you. You showed me that there was rest in the mourning of letting go and moving as you became this beautiful composition of broken that I'd fallen in love with. I wrote all of these books as a dedication to the woman you were and to the woman you have become in hopes of reaching individuals who know exactly how it feels to be in the shoes of someone as powerful and significant as you. Someone who has had to fight through the storms and continue on a lonely path that would lead you to a better understanding of self and to a love that was worthy of your attention. Thank you for being my muse. Thank you for loving me as if you've never been hurt. Thank you for saying "I DO."

You're so hard-pressed to find someone who cares that you seem to be holding on tight to people who never will. You're so eager for love that you let anyone in and they continue to hurt you. Maybe it's time to stop giving yourself away to people who are not interested in making an effort. Maybe it's time to stop entrusting your heart to disloyal and unclean hands.

You're so much more than they would lead you to believe. You're so much greater than the relationship you've settled for. You're not a welcome mat for pain. You were not designed to be someone's emotional punching bag. You are more than they'd want you to believe. Do not listen to others as they attempt to define you in ways that would suggest that you deserve to be unhappy. They don't know you like you know yourself. Do not allow them the power to make you forget who you truly are.

she felt like feeling nothing
she just wants to forget . . .

you felt like feeling nothing
you just want to forget
but in the end and though
this is where we part ways
i hope you, the reader
the one who has chosen
to consume these words . . .

i hope you remember me
and all the things i've said . . .

you are worth it . . .
(message complete . . .)

Index

Andrews McMeel Publishing
a division of Andrews McMeel Universal
1130 Walnut Street, Kansas City, Missouri 64106

www.andrewsmcmeel.com

19 20 21 22 23 SDB 10 9 8 7 6 5 4 3 2 1

ISBN: 978-1-4494-9754-5

Library of Congress Control Number: 2018961641

Editor: Patty Rice
Designer/Art Director: Diane Marsh
Production Editor: Dave Shaw
Production Manager: Cliff Koehler

attention: schools and businesses

Andrews McMeel books are available at quantity discounts
with bulk purchase for educational, business, or sales
promotional use. For information, please e-mail the Andrews
McMeel Publishing Special Sales Department:
specialsales@amuniversal.com.